AIR MAGIC!

Because air is invisible, you may forget that it is all around us all of the time. But there's magic in the air, and each trick reveals another of its amazing qualities. Air is made up of many gases which are essential to life on Earth. It can squeeze itself into very small spaces and expand when its heated. Air can move around, and even has the power to support other objects. Its a magnificent, show-stopping magic prop.

BE AN EXPERT MAGICIAN

PREPARING YOUR ROUTINE

There is much more to being a magician than just doing tricks. It is important that you and your assistant practise your whole routine lots of times, so that your performance goes smoothly when you do it for real. You will be a more entertaining magician if you do.

PROPS

Props are all the bits and pieces of equipment that a magician uses during an act. This includes your clothes as well as the tricks themselves. It's a good idea to make a magician's trunk from a large box to keep all your props in. During your routine, you can dip into the trunk, pulling out all sorts of equipment and crazy objects (see Distraction). You could tell jokes about these objects.

PROPS LIST

Magic wand	Silver foil	
Top hat	Sticky-putty	
Waistcoat	Wax candle	
Silk scarves	Marbles	
Balloons	Cardboard	
Paint	Eggs	
Boxes	Straws	Rubber bands
Plastic tubes	Ping-pong balls	Coins
Containers	Polystyrene	Sticky-tape

SCIENCE

MAGIC
WITH AIR

CHRIS OXLADE

GLOUCESTER PRESS
LONDON • NEW YORK • TORONTO • SYDNEY

Design
David West Children's Book
Design
Designer
Steve Woosnam Savage
Editor
Suzanne Melia
Illustrator
Ian Thompson
Model maker
Keith Newell
Photographer
Roger Vlitos

© Aladdin Books Ltd 1993
Created and designed by
N.W. Books
28 Percy Street
London W1P 9FF

First published in
Great Britain in 1993 by
Franklin Watts Ltd
96 Leonard Street
London EC2A 4RH

ISBN 0 7496 1312 2

A CIP catalogue record for this
book is available from the British
Library

Printed in Belgium.

CONTENTS

WHICH TRICKS?

Work out which tricks you want to put in your routine. Put in some long tricks and some short tricks. This will keep your audience interested. If you can, include a trick that you can keep going back to during the routine. Magicians call this a "running gag".

MAGICIAN'S PATTER

Patter is what you say during your routine. Good patter makes a routine much more interesting and allows it to run much more smoothly. It is a good way to entertain your audience during

DISTRACTION

Distraction is an important part of a magician's routine. By waving a colourful scarf in the air and telling a joke, you can take the audience's attention away from something you'd rather they didn't see!

KEEP IT SECRET

The best magicians never give away their secrets. If anyone asks how your tricks work, just reply "By magic!" Then you can impress people with your tricks again and again.

the slower times in your routine. Try to make up a story for each trick. Remember to introduce yourself and your assistant at the start and to thank the audience at the end. Practise your patter when you practise your tricks.

INTRODUCING MAGIC MANDY
AND THE
SELF-INFLATING BALLOON

The balloon inflates by itself as
Magic Mandy has a fit of sneezing!

Reach beneath your magic table and pretend
to take hold of a balloon. As you do, secretly
pull the balloon from one sleeve and the
tube from the other. Hide the tube by
picking up the handkerchief. Now
pretend to sneeze into the
handkerchief (but secretly blow into
the tube) and the balloon will inflate!

WHAT YOU NEED
Plastic tubing
Balloons
Elastic bands
Silk handkerchief

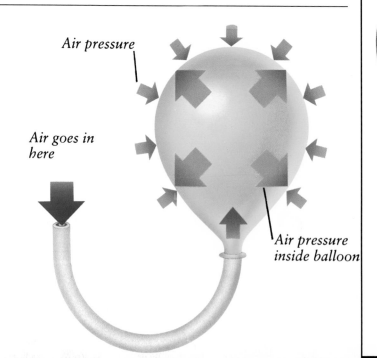

THE SCIENCE
BEHIND THE TRICK

When you blow out, the
air is squeezed inside your
lungs. This increases the
pressure of the air, making
it higher than the pressure
inside the balloon. Air
always moves from an area
of high pressure to an area
of low pressure, so it
rushes along the tube to
the balloon. A balloon is
difficult to inflate because
you have to stretch the
rubber using the air
pressure in your lungs.

Air pressure

*Air goes in
here*

*Air pressure
inside balloon*

8

1 Cut a piece of plastic tubing long enough to go up one sleeve, around your back and down the other sleeve.

2 Stretch the neck of a balloon over one end of the tube. If it's loose, wind an elastic band tightly around it. Feed the tube along your sleeves.

3 Put elastic bands around your wrists (not too tightly) to hold the tube in place.

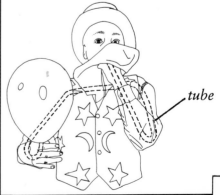

tube

9

INTRODUCING MAGIC MALCOLM
AND THE
JUMPING COIN TRICK

Magic Mike makes the coin jump in an amazing feat of mind over matter.

Let your audience inspect the coin and the bottle to prove that there is nothing "tricky" about them. Put the coin over the neck of the bottle (remember to wet it secretly first). Now put your hands gently on either side of the bottle and the coin will begin to jump!

WHAT YOU NEED
Large plastic drinks bottle
Small coin
Dish of water

THE SCIENCE BEHIND THE TRICK

Your hands are warmer than the bottle and the air inside it. Heat always flows from a warmer place to a cooler place. When you put your hands on the sides of the bottle, heat flows from your hands into the bottle and warms the air. When air gets hotter, its tiny particles, molecules, move about faster as it expands. The water seals the area around the coin to stop air leaking out. The expanding warm air breaks the seal and the coin flips up to let some air escape. The coin falls back down until the air expands again.

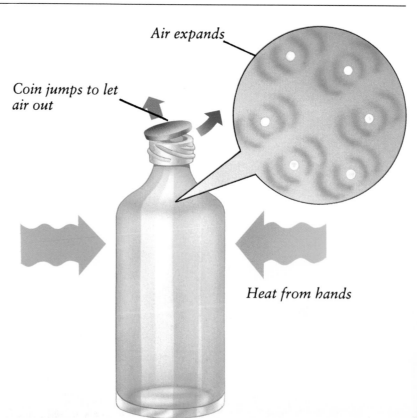

Air expands

Coin jumps to let air out

Heat from hands

10

1 Paint the bottle with oil-based paint. Find a coin which just covers the neck of the bottle. You will also need a small dish of water. Keep this hidden away and dip the coin in it just before you perform the trick.

INTRODUCING MAGIC MARCIA
AND THE
HOVERCRAFT TRICK

Only Magic Marcia has the power to make this strange craft float along.

Put the hovercraft in the centre of your table. Invite members of your audience to come forward and try to move the craft by blowing. It will refuse to move. Ask your volunteers to stand back. Now blow sharply into the top of the hovercraft and it will glide smoothly across the table!

WHAT YOU NEED
Plastic bottle
Coloured card
Sticky putty

THE SCIENCE
BEHIND THE TRICK

It's difficult to blow the hovercraft along because of friction between its "skirt" and the table. When you blow into the hole in the top, air gets squeezed inside. This makes a "cushion" of air underneath which lifts the hovercraft off the table so that it can float along.

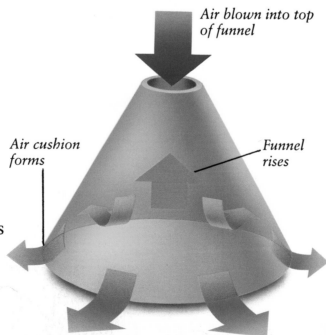

Air blown into top of funnel

Air cushion forms

Funnel rises

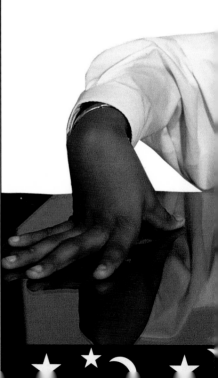

1 Cut off the top 5 or 6 cm of a plastic bottle.

3 Fold the skirt around the bottle top and glue it into place.

2 Now make a "skirt" to fit over the bottle top. Cut a semi-circle of card and decorate it as shown.

4 If the hovercraft moves too easily, add some sticky putty underneath.

INTRODUCING MAGIC MALCOLM
AND THE
ROLLING BALL TRICK

Magic Malcolm's wand focuses the mind power of the audience to make the mysterious ball roll.

Rest your hand on top of the container and point your wand at the ball. Tell the audience that they can move the ball just by mind power. Ask them to look at the ball and concentrate hard. Secretly press the balloon and they will think they are moving the ball!

WHAT YOU NEED
Spray can lid
Large glass jar or beaker
Balloons
Sticky tape
Marble
Card

 ## THE SCIENCE
BEHIND THE TRICK

Air is trapped inside both the containers. When you press on the balloon, the air inside the large container gets squeezed. Its pressure goes up. Now the pressure outside the small container is greater than inside. The air outside pushes the balloon on the small container inwards and the ball rolls down the slope.

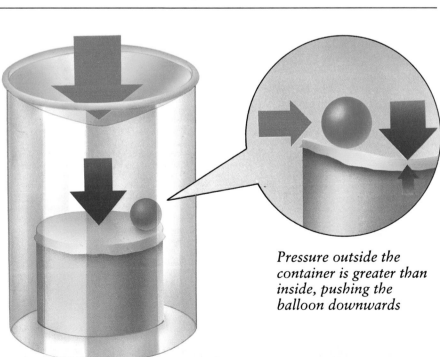

Pressure outside the container is greater than inside, pushing the balloon downwards

14

1 Find a plastic lid about 4 cm across. Make sure that there are no holes in it because it needs to be airtight.

2 Cut the neck off a balloon. Stretch it over the lid so that it's tight, like a drum. Tape around the edges to keep the balloon in place.

3 Now find a large, strong glass container (e.g. a coffee jar). Make sure that its big enough to hold the lid.

4 Decorate the lid and put it in the glass container with the ball on top. Seal the glass container by stretching another balloon over the top. This is the part that you will press.

INTRODUCING MAGIC MIKE
AND THE
MAGIC HELICOPTER

No motor? That's no matter to Magic Mike as he makes the helicopter work by magic.

Put the helicopter on the cylinder without the jar inside and put the rotor on. The rotor will stay still. Now move the helicopter to the other cylinder and wave your wand. This time the rotor will turn — and keep turning! Make this the first trick in your routine and the rotor will still be turning at the end.

WHAT YOU NEED
Card
Large needle
Silver foil
Jar

THE SCIENCE BEHIND THE TRICK

The water in the jar gives off heat, which warms the air around it. The tiny particles in the air (called molecules) move about faster, which makes the air expand and become less dense. The warm, light air floats upwards in the cool, heavier air around it, just as light things float in water. The stream of warm air flows out of the cylinder, making a light wind which moves the rotor. The rotor keeps going until all the heat in the water is used up and the air around it stops being warmed.

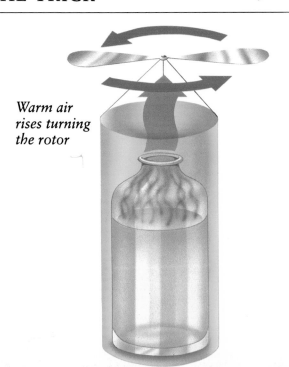

Warm air rises turning the rotor

16

GETTING PREPARED

1 Copy a helicopter shape onto card and cut it out. Tape a large needle to the back with the point at the top.

2 Cut a rotor shape out of silver foil. Shape it so that it balances on the pin. Make two cylinders of about 30 cm high from card.

3 Just before your routine, put a jar of warm water into one of the cylinders.

INTRODUCING MAGIC MARCIA
AND THE
SINKING SQUID

Going up! Going down! The little squid sinks at Magic Marcia's command.

This trick gives you a good opportunity for some funny patter. Perhaps you could start with "This squid has baffled the world's greatest scientists ..." Squeeze the bottle to make the squid sink and let go again to make it float!

WHAT YOU NEED
Paper clips
Bendy straws
Sticky putty
Plastic
Large plastic drinks bottle

THE SCIENCE BEHIND THE TRICK

When you squeeze the bottle, you are trying to squeeze the water and air inside. The water cannot be squashed, but the air can. The air inside the model is squashed or compressed. This lets more water in, making the squid heavier and it sinks.

Pressure

Water enters the model

The model sinks

18

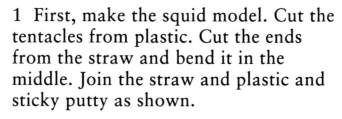

1 First, make the squid model. Cut the tentacles from plastic. Cut the ends from the straw and bend it in the middle. Join the straw and plastic and sticky putty as shown.

2 Stick an undersea scene on the bottle. Add or remove sticky putty until the squid just floats. Fill the bottle with water, put in the squid and put on the cap.

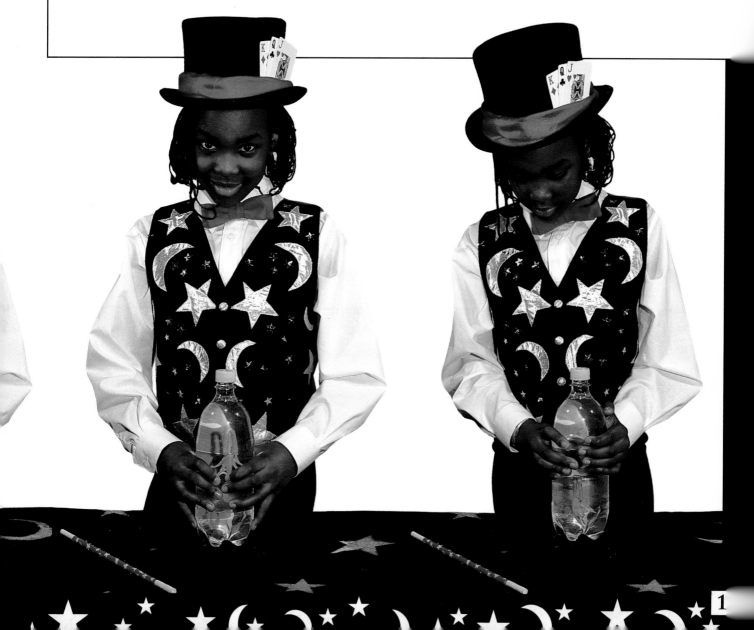

1

INTRODUCING MAGIC MARCIA
AND THE
HOVERING BALL TRICK

The ball seems to be attached to the end of Magic Marcia's wand by an invisible force!

Hold the ball above the centre of the box while your assistant secretly pushes the vacuum hose into the hole. Now move the ball by saying "left" or "right". Your assistant listens and moves the hose so that it looks as though the ball is under your control. At the end of the trick, your assistant pulls the hose away very quickly and you show the empty box.

THINGS YOU NEED
Ping-pong ball
Large cardboard box
Vacuum cleaner (must be able to blow as well as suck)

THE SCIENCE
BEHIND THE TRICK

The stream of air pushes the ball into the air. The air flows all around the ball as it hovers. If the ball moves sideways, more air flows around one side than the other. This creates a pull on the ball and it returns to the centre of the stream. It works a bit like an aircraft wing. It even works when the stream of air is at an angle.

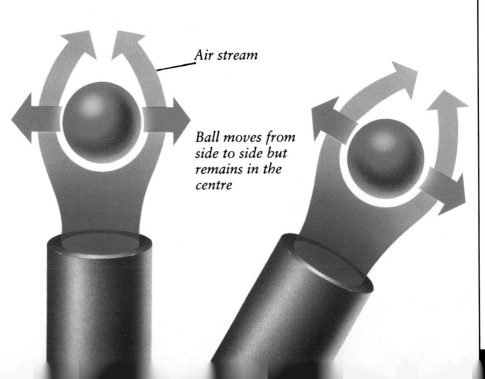

Air stream

Ball moves from side to side but remains in the centre

1. Find and decorate a large cardboard box. Cut a slot in the back large enough for the cleaner's hose to fit through.

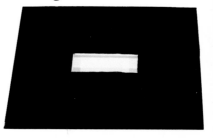

2. Put the cleaner into blowing mode. Before your routine, hide the cleaner under your magic table, with your assistant.

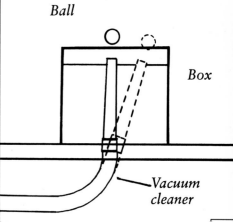

Ball

Box

Vacuum cleaner

INTRODUCING MAGIC MARK
AND THE
NON-BURSTING BALLOON

Magic Mark astounds the audience with a trick that doesn't go off with a bang!

Pick up one of your prepared balloons and show it to the audience. The sticky tape will be almost impossible to see. Now push a pin into the balloon through the sticky tape. Your audience will probably flinch because they think the balloon is going to burst! Take out the pin and quickly burst the balloon to destroy the evidence.

WHAT YOU NEED
Balloons
Sticky tape
Pins

THE SCIENCE
BEHIND THE TRICK

When a balloon is blown up, the rubber is very stretched. Inside the balloon, the air is squeezed tight. When you stick in a pin, you start a tear in the rubber. Faster than the eye can see, the tear spreads and all the air rushes out, making a bang. The sticky tape stops the tear from spreading.

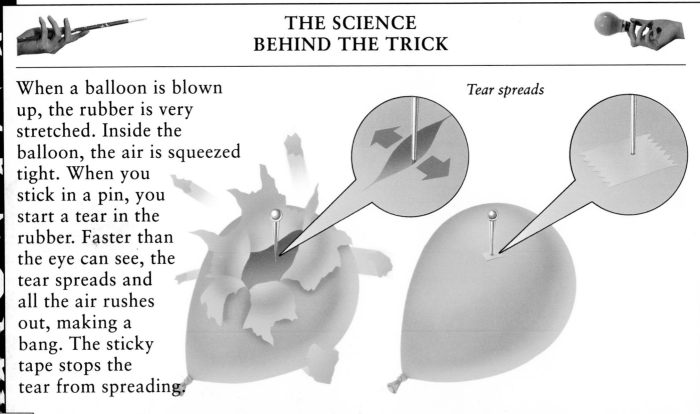

Tear spreads

This trick is quick and easy to prepare for. It's best to prepare two or three special balloons just in case things go a bit wrong! Blow up each balloon and tie the neck. Cut a piece of sticky tape about 2 cm long and stick it near the top of the balloon. Smooth it down carefully so that it's difficult to see.

INTRODUCING MAGIC MANDY
AND THE
RISING TIDE TRICK

Even the ebb and flow of the tide is under Magic Mandy's spell!

WHAT YOU NEED
Large glass container
Glass jar
Small coins
Party candles
Polystyrene

Slowly pour the water into a large container. Float the boat above the coins and light the candle. Announce that you will make the tide rise under the boat. Place the jar over the boat so that it rests on the coins. The water will begin to rise!

THE SCIENCE BEHIND THE TRICK

When something burns, it uses up oxygen in the air. In fact, without oxygen, things cannot burn at all. When you put the jar over the boat, the oxygen inside is gradually used up. The air pressure on the water in the large container pushes water up into the jar. The candle goes out because there is no more oxygen for burning.

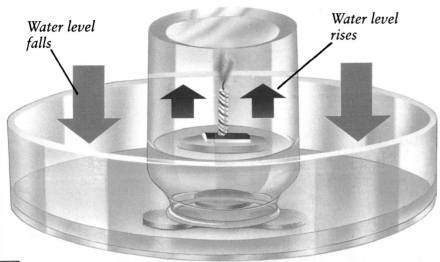

Water level falls

Water level rises

1 Find a large glass container. The one shown here is ideal. If you don't have a glass container, you can use a shallow tray or a large plate.

2 Put three small coins in the middle of the tray and space them out so that they support the upturned jar. Pour some water into a jug.

3 Cut out two pieces of polystyrene, as shown, and stick them together to make a boat. Place a small candle in the top.

INTRODUCING MAGIC MALCOLM
AND THE
ASTONISHING EGG

And finally... Magic Malcolm has his audience diving for cover with another egg-citing trick!

This trick gives you a good opportunity for some funny patter. Perhaps you could start "These are the rare and valuable eggs of an extinct bird ..." Open the egg box, take out an egg and throw it hard at the ceiling. Your audience will think they are about to be covered in egg, but a parachute will float down instead.

WHAT YOU NEED
Silk handkerchief
Modelling clay
String
Eggs
Egg box

THE SCIENCE
BEHIND THE TRICK

When an object falls through the air, the air tries to slow it down. This is called drag or air resistance. When the parachute begins to fall, the drag on the weight is much less than on the handkerchief. The weight falls faster, pulling the parachute open. When the parachute is open, its drag is much greater so it slows down and floats to the ground.

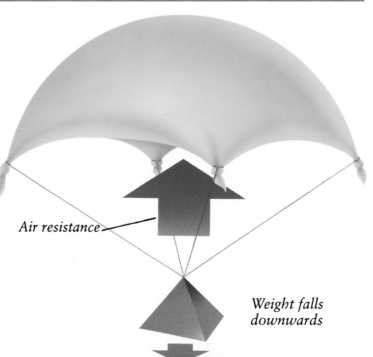

Air resistance

Weight falls downwards

26

GETTING PREPARED

2 Tie a piece of string to each corner of the handkerchief. Fold a piece of modelling clay around the strings.

1 Using a pin, carefully make a small hole in the end of an egg. Gradually make the hole bigger and wash out the white and yoke.

3 Carefully push the parachute into the egg. Be careful not to tangle the strings. Decorate an egg box to keep your eggs in.

HINTS AND TIPS

Here are some hints and tips for making your props. Good props will make your act look more professional. So spend time making and decorating your props, and look after them carefully. As well as the special props you need for each trick, try to make some general props such as a waistcoat and magic wand.

Decorate your props with magic shapes cut from coloured paper. Paint bottles and tubes with oil-based paint.

You will need sticky-tape and glue to make props. Double-sided tape might also be useful. You can use sticky putty or special plastic sealant to make water-proof joints.

Try cutting magic shapes out of card and using the holes to make stencils.

Your act will look extra professional if you make a proper stage set. This is easy if you have a backcloth to hang behind the stage. A large piece of black cloth would be most effective. Use silver paint to create stars and moons. Decorate pieces of cloth to throw over your table. The overall effect should be a set that creates an atmosphere of mystery and magic.

Make your own magician's clothes. Try to find an old hat and waistcoat to decorate. If you can find some silvery material, cut out stars and moons and sew them on. An alternative is sequins. Use anything that is shiney and dramatic so you look professional.

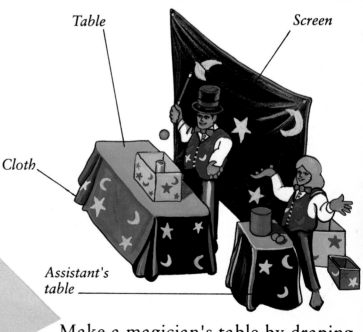

Table

Screen

Cloth

Assistant's table

Make a magician's table by draping a cloth over a table. You can put the props underneath out of sight.

GLOSSARY

AIR PRESSURE The force exerted on the surface of objects due to the squeezing or pressing of air.

AIR RESISTANCE The drag or resistance that air exerts on falling objects. The larger the surface area of an object, the greater the air resistance.

BURNING The use of oxygen in the air to release heat energy from certain materials.

COMPRESSION The squeezing together of particles as a substance moves into a smaller space. As air is compressed, it exerts a higher pressure on the surrounding container.

FRICTION A force between two objects that rub together, slowing things down. Air can sometimes act as a lubricant, reducing the friction between two surfaces.

MOLECULES The smallest naturally occurring particles of a substance.

OXYGEN A gas without taste, colour or smell that forms a part of air. It is essential to life on Earth.

INDEX